EASY PIANO
BEATLES GREATEST HITS

ISBN 978-0-7935-0047-5

HAL•LEONARD
CORPORATION
7777 W. BLUEMOUND RD. P.O. BOX 13819 MILWAUKEE, WI 53213

CONTENTS

CAN'T BUY ME LOVE

Words and Music by JOHN LENNON
and PAUL McCARTNEY

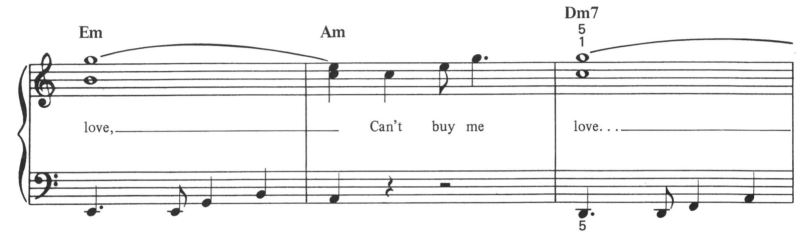

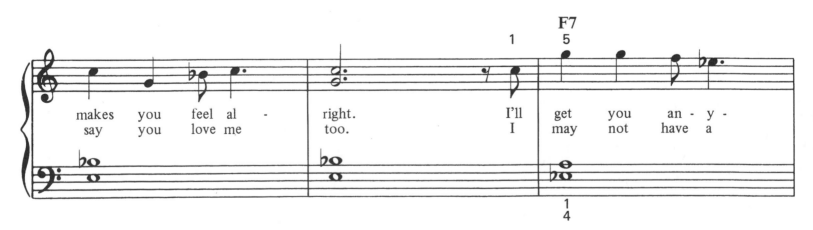

thing, my friend, if it makes you feel al - right. 'Cause
lot to give, but what I've got I'll give to you.

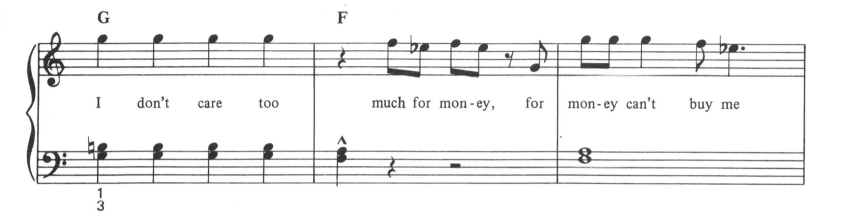

I don't care too much for mon - ey, for mon - ey can't buy me

love. I'll love. Can't buy me love,

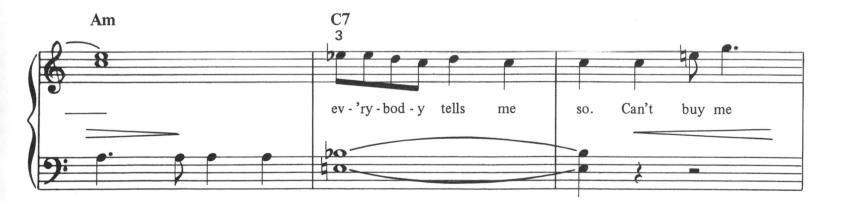

ev - 'ry - bod - y tells me so. Can't buy me

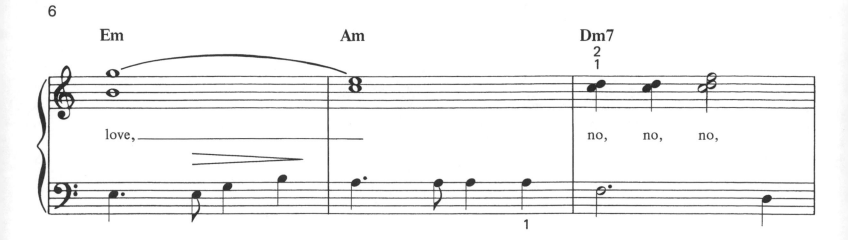

Em — love, _____ **Am** — **Dm7** no, no, no,

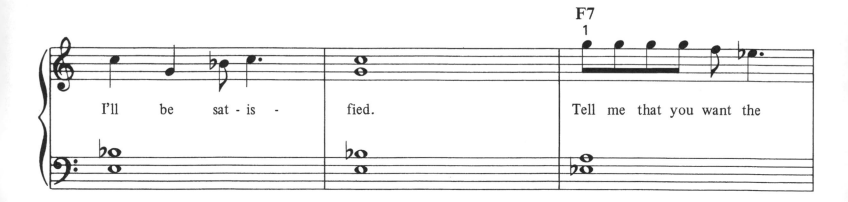

G no! **C7** 3. Say you don't need no dia - mond rings and *mf*

I'll be sat - is - fied. **F7** Tell me that you want the

C7 kind of things that mon - ey just can't buy.

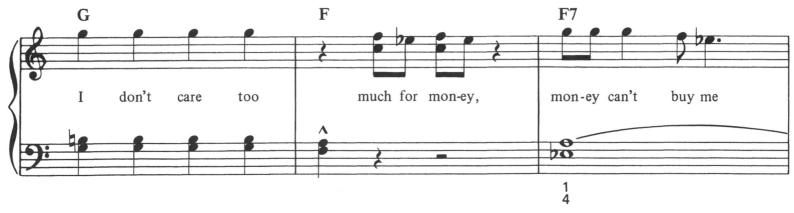

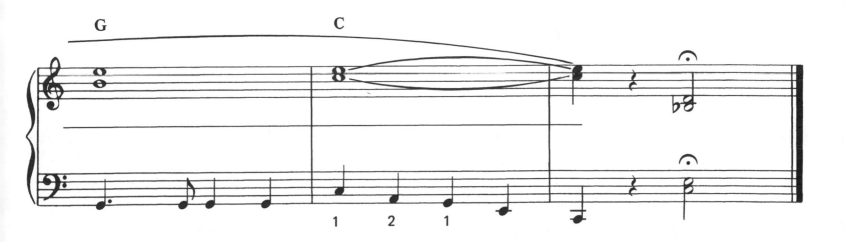

ALL YOU NEED IS LOVE

Words and Music by JOHN LENNON
and PAUL McCARTNEY

Moderately, not too fast

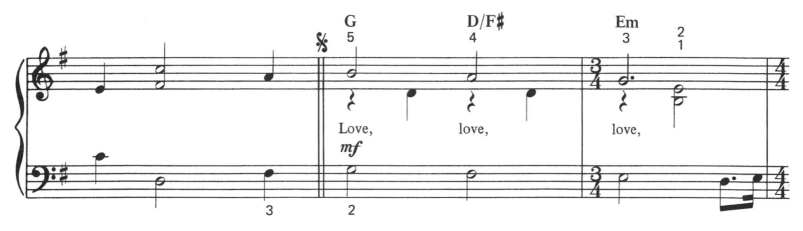

Love, love, love,

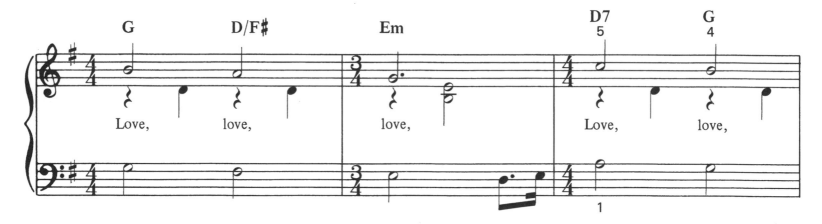

Love, love, love, Love, love,

love...

There's noth-ing you can do that can't be done.
Noth-ing you can make that can't be made.
Noth-ing you can know that is - n't known.

Noth-ing you can sing that can't be sung.
No one you can save that can't be saved.
Noth-ing you can see that is - n't shown.

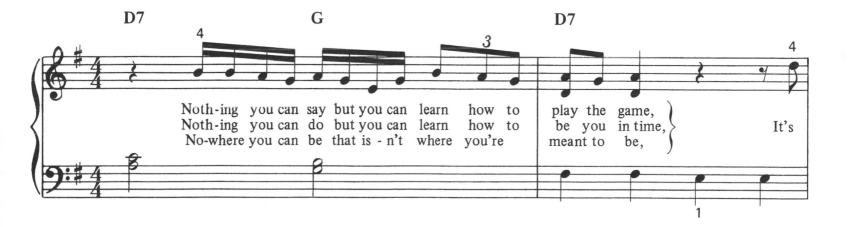

Noth-ing you can say but you can learn how to play the game,
Noth-ing you can do but you can learn how to be you in time,
No-where you can be that is - n't where you're meant to be,

It's

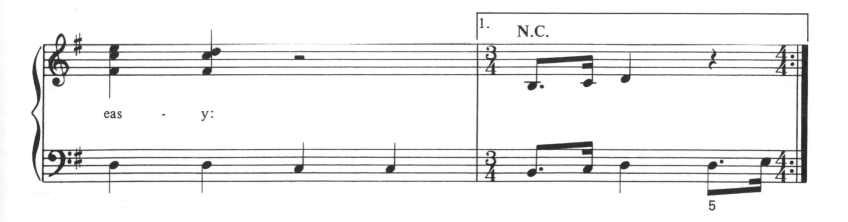

eas - y:

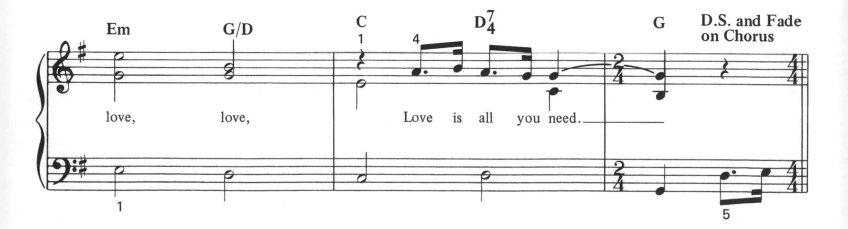

COME TOGETHER

Words and Music by JOHN LENNON
and PAUL McCARTNEY

Slow and funky

G7

Got to be a jok-er, he just do what he please.

Dm7

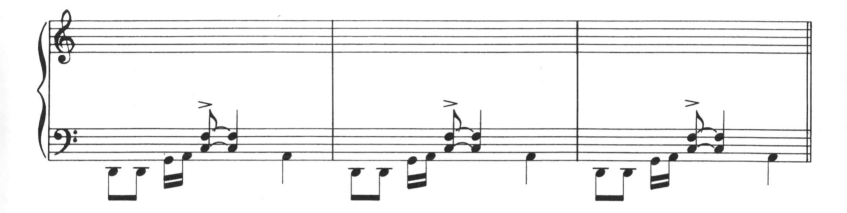

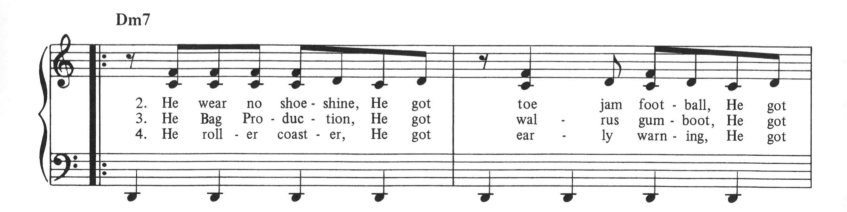

Dm7

2. He wear no shoe-shine, He got
3. He Bag Pro-duc-tion, He got
4. He roll-er coast-er, He got

toe jam foot-ball, He got
wal-rus gum-boot, He got
ear-ly warn-ing, He got

mon-key fin-ger, He shoot
O-no side-board, He one
Mud-dy Wa-ter, He one

Co-ca Co-la, He say,
spi-nal crack-er, He got
Mo-jo fil-ter, He say,

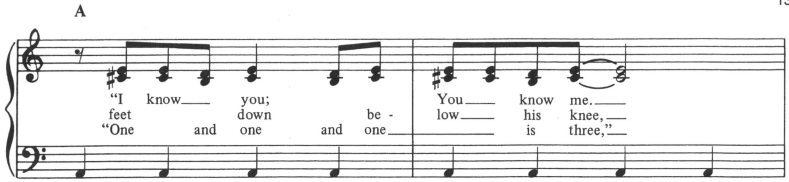

A

"I know____ you; You____ know me.____
feet down be - low____ his knee,____
"One and one and one____ is three,"

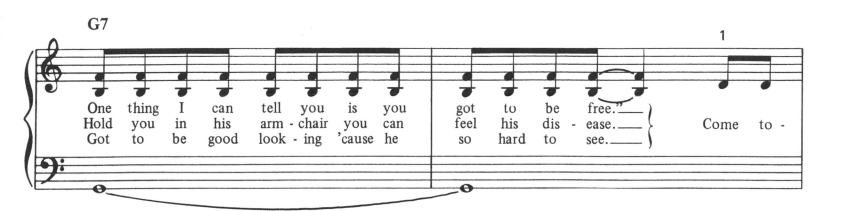

G7

One thing I can tell you is you got to be free."____ } Come to-
Hold you in his arm - chair you can feel his dis - ease.____
Got to be good look - ing 'cause he so hard to see.____

1

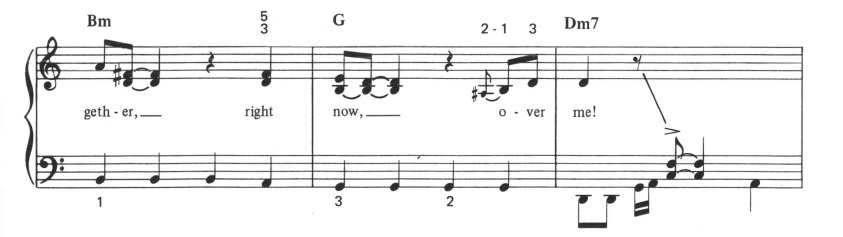

Bm — **5/3** — **G** — **2 - 1 3** — **Dm7**

geth - er,____ right now,____ o - ver me!

1 — **3** — **2**

**After 4th verse,
D.C. and fade**

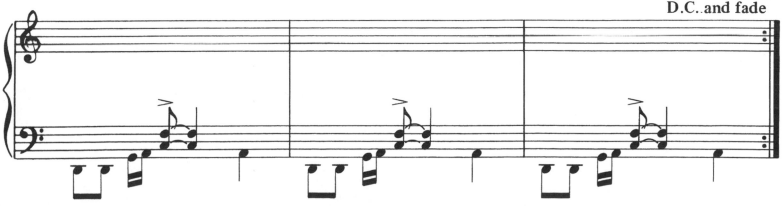

DAY TRIPPER

Words and Music by JOHN LENNON
and PAUL McCARTNEY

Got a good rea - son
She's a big teas - er,
Tried to please her,

for

tak - ing the eas - y way out;
she took me half the way out there;
she on - ly played one night stands;

Got a good rea - son
She's a big teas - er,
Tried to please her,

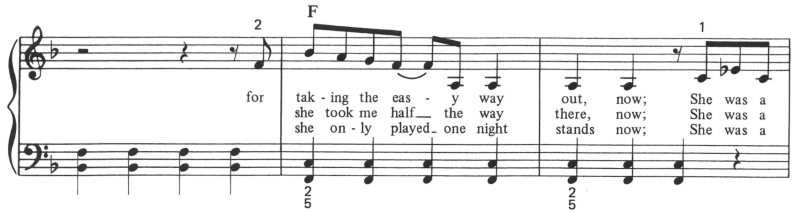

for taking the eas - y way out, now; She was a
she took me half__ the way there, now; She was a
she on - ly played__ one night stands now; She was a

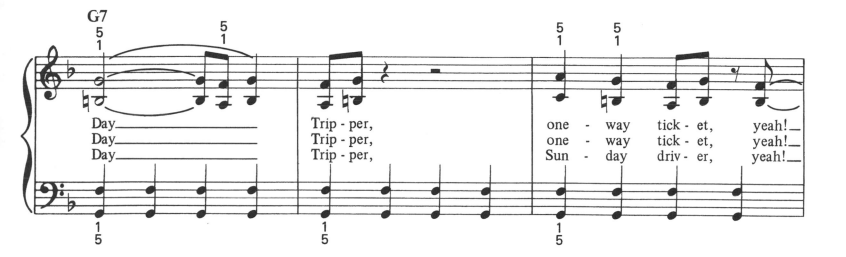

Day_____ Trip - per, one - way tick - et, yeah!__
Day_____ Trip - per, one - way tick - et, yeah!__
Day_____ Trip - per, Sun - day driv - er, yeah!__

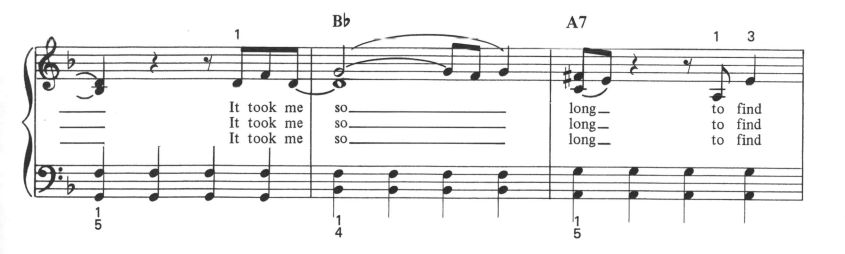

____ It took me so_____ long__ to find
____ It took me so_____ long__ to find
____ It took me so_____ long__ to find

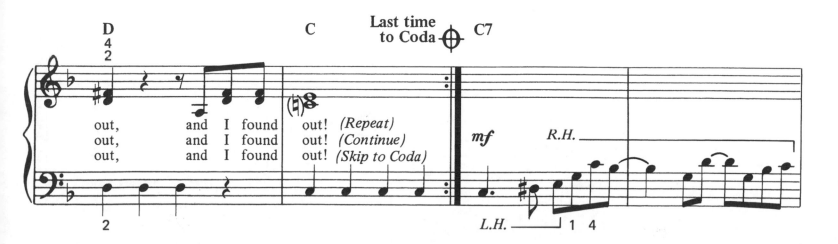

out, and I found out! *(Repeat)*
out, and I found out! *(Continue)*
out, and I found out! *(Skip to Coda)*

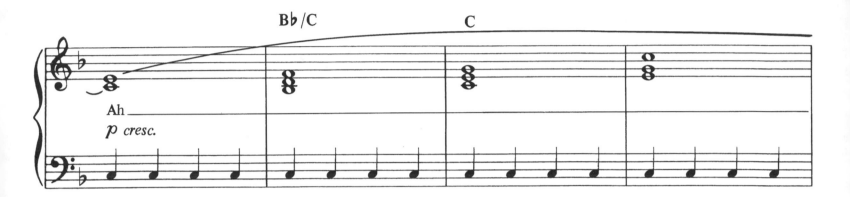

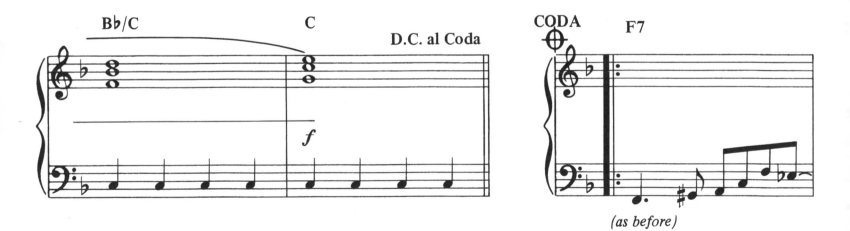

EIGHT DAYS A WEEK

Words and Music by JOHN LENNON
and PAUL McCARTNEY

Brightly, in 4

Ooh I need your love, babe, guess you know it's true;
Love you ev - 'ry day, babe, al - ways on my mind;

Hope you need my love, babe, just like I need you.
One thing I can say, girl, love you all the time.

Hold me, — love me, — hold me, — love me, — I

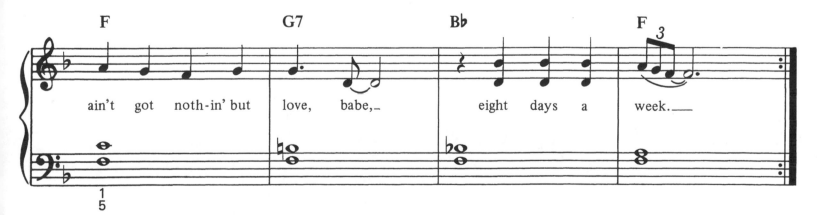

ain't got noth-in' but love, babe, eight days a week. —

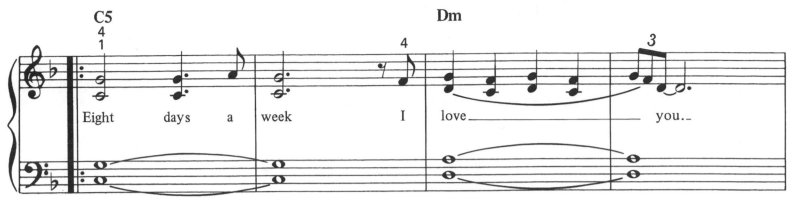

Eight days a week I love you.

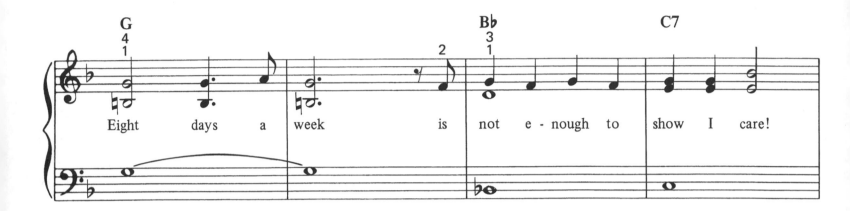

Eight days a week is not e - nough to show I care!

Ooh I need your love, babe, guess you know it's true;
Love you ev - 'ry day, babe, girl, al - ways on my mind;

Hope you need my love, babe, just like I need you.
One thing I can say, girl, love you all the time.

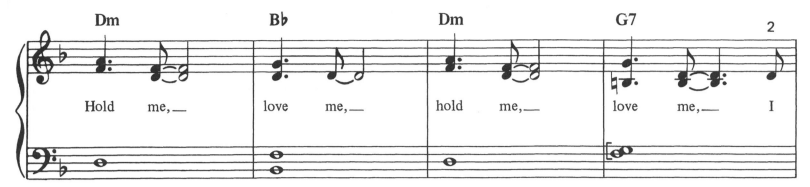

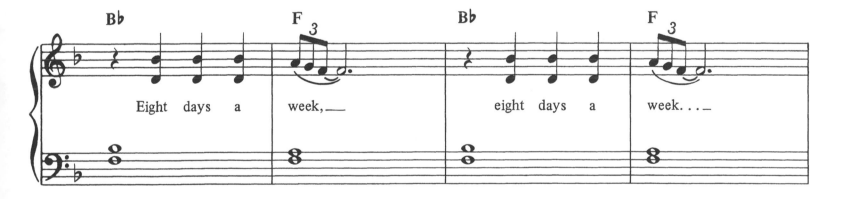

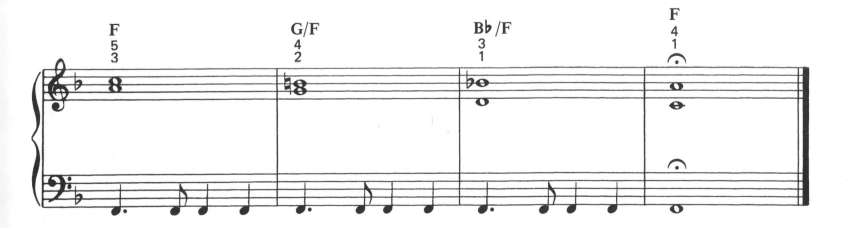

ELEANOR RIGBY

Words and Music by JOHN LENNON
and PAUL McCARTNEY

Moderately, with a steady beat

Ah,_____ look at all___ the lone - ly peo -

- ple!___

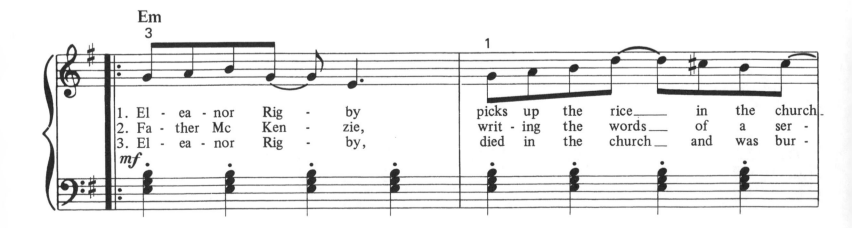

1. El - ea - nor Rig - by   picks up the rice___ in the church
2. Fa - ther Mc Ken - zie,   writ - ing the words___ of a ser -
3. El - ea - nor Rig - by,   died in the church___ and was bur -

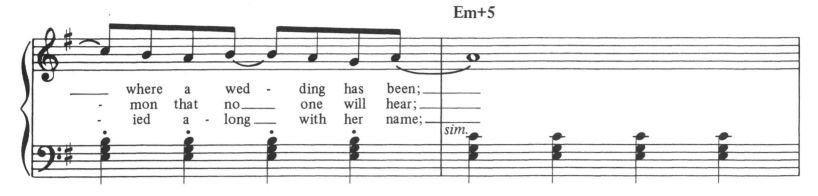

where a wed - ding has been;
- mon that no____ one will hear;
- ied a - long____ with her name;____

Lives in a dream.____
No one comes near.____
No - bod - y came.____

Waits at the win - dow,
Look at him work - ing,
Fa - ther Mc Ken - zie,

wear - ing the face____ that she keeps____
darn - ing his socks____ in the night____
wip - ing the dirt____ from his hands____

in a jar____ by the door;____
when there's no - bod - y there;____
as he walks____ from the grave;____

Who is it for?____
What does he care?____
No one was saved.____

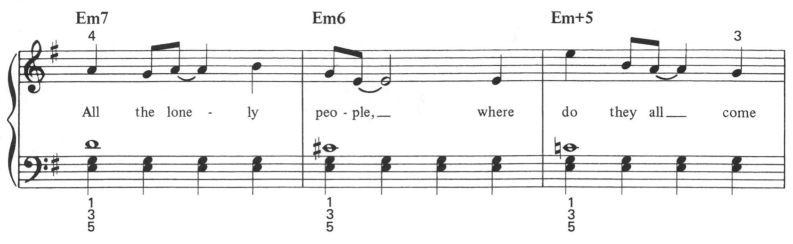

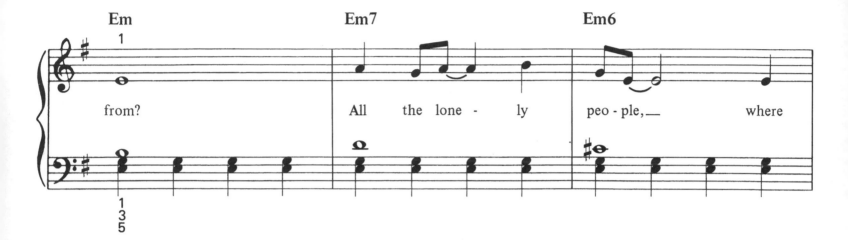

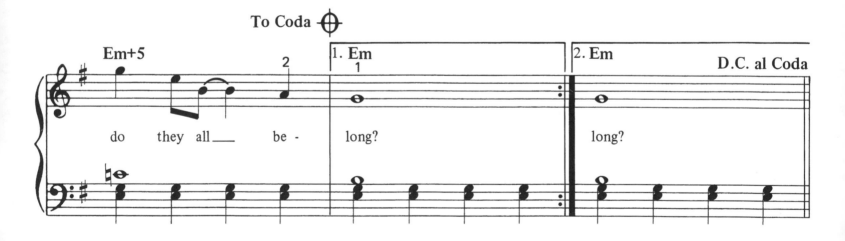

HELLO, GOODBYE

Words and Music by JOHN LENNON
and PAUL McCARTNEY

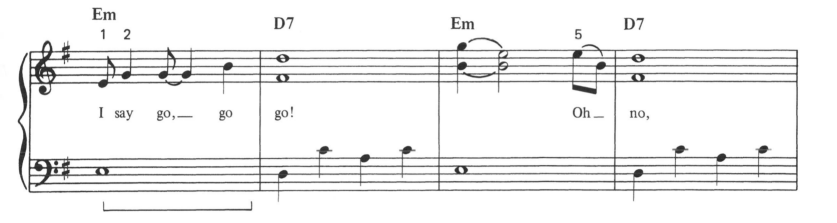

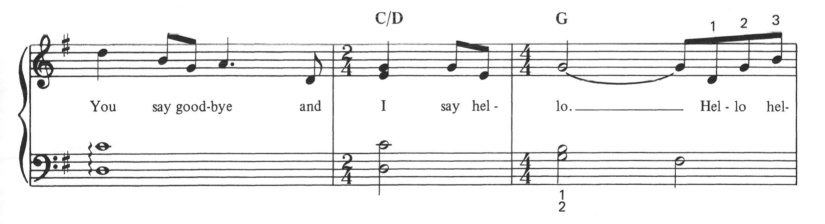

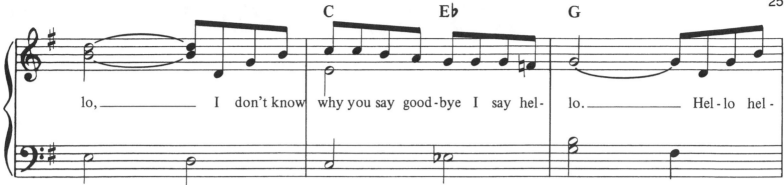

lo, _____ I don't know why you say good-bye I say hel- lo. _____ Hel-lo hel-

lo, _____ I don't know why you say good-bye I say hel- lo.

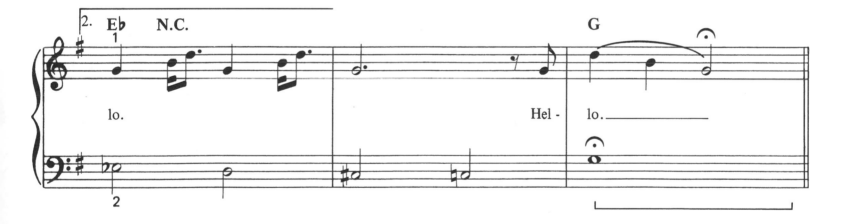

lo. Hel - lo. _____

Repeat and Fade

Hel - lo, _____ he - ba _ hel - lo - a...

A HARD DAY'S NIGHT

Words and Music by JOHN LENNON
and PAUL McCARTNEY

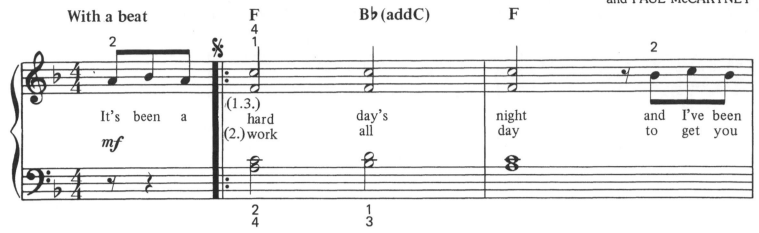

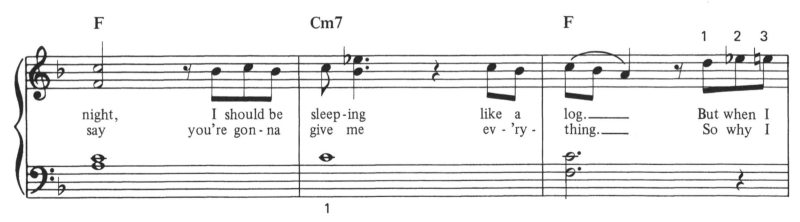

3rd time to Coda ⊕

1.

2.

F   Bb7   F   F   Am

feel_ al - right.   You know I
be_ O._

K.   When I'm   home

Dm   Am   F

ev-'ry-thing seems_ to be   al - right,   When I'm   home

D.S. al Coda   **CODA** ⊕

Dm   Bb   C   N.C.   F

feel-ing you hold-ing me   tight.   Yeah! It's been a   right,   You know I

Bb7   F   Bb(addC)   F

feel_ al -   right,   You know I   feel   al -   right.

HEY JUDE

Words and Music by JOHN LENNON
and PAUL McCARTNEY

Slow and steady

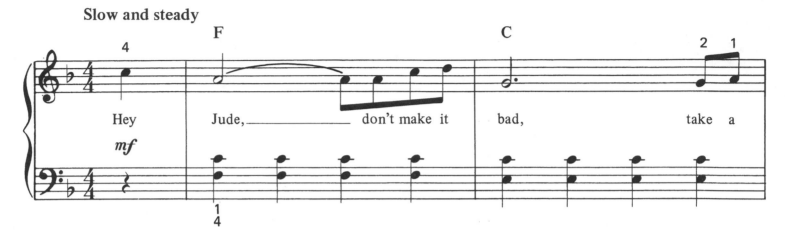

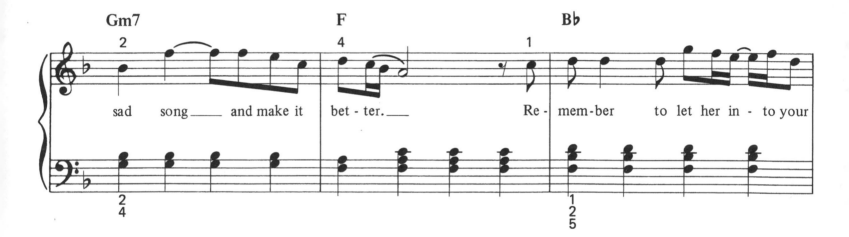

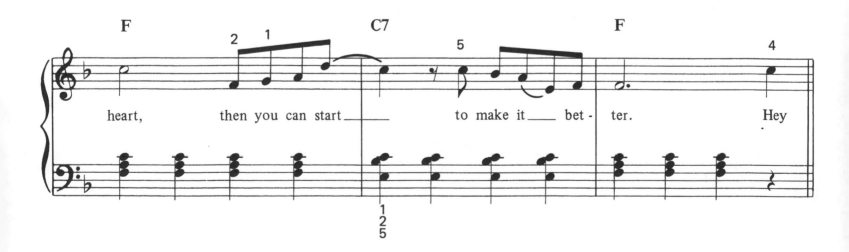

Jude,_____ don't be a - fraid; You were made to____ go out and
Jude,_____ don't let me down; You have found her,____ now go and

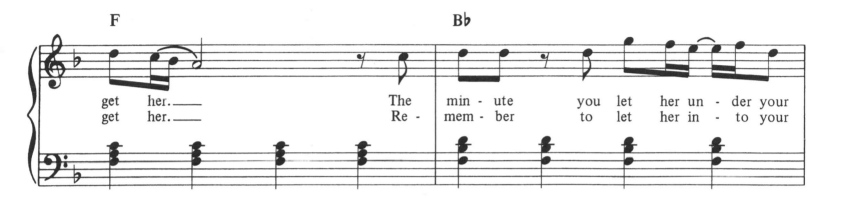

get her.____ The
get her.____ Re - mem - ber you let her un - der your
mi - nute to let her in - to your

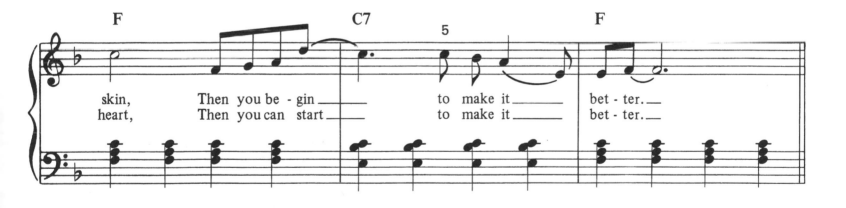

skin, Then you be - gin____ to make it____ bet - ter.____
heart, Then you can start____ to make it____ bet - ter.____

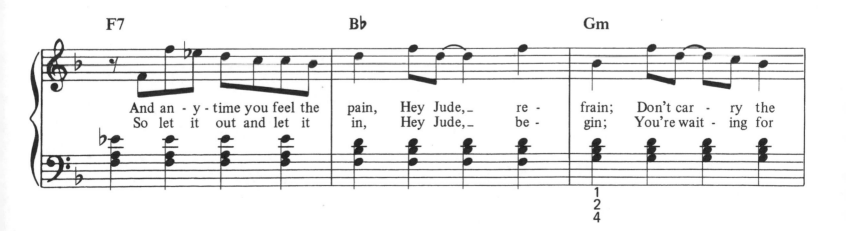

And an - y - time you feel the pain, Hey Jude,__ re - frain; Don't car - ry the
So let it out and let it in, Hey Jude,__ be - gin; You're wait - ing for

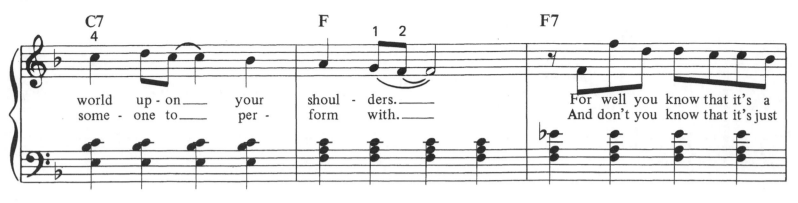

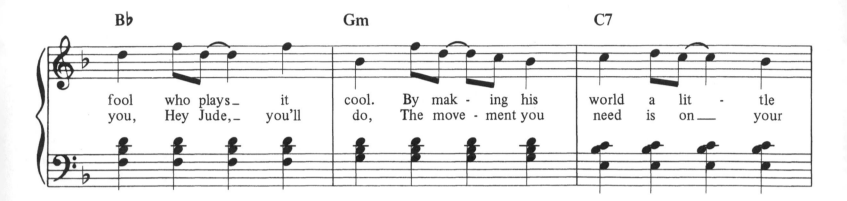

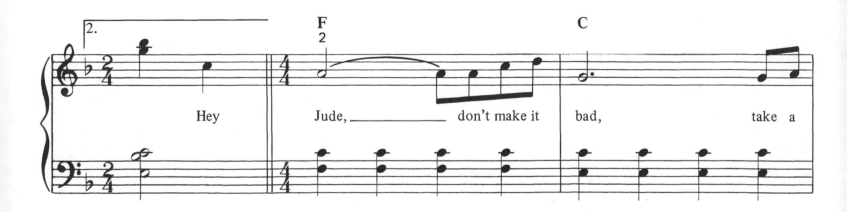

sad song___ and make it bet - ter.___ Re -

mem-ber to let her un - der your skin, then you'll be - gin___ to make it

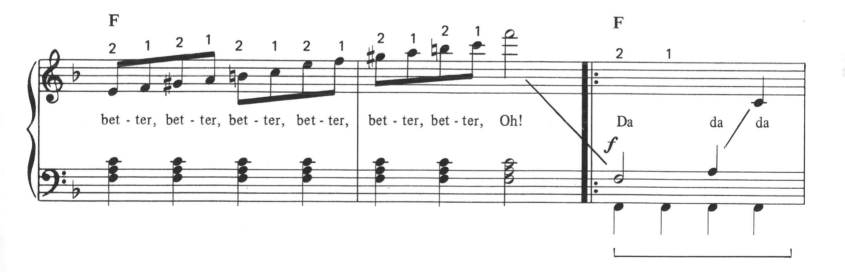

bet - ter, bet - ter, bet - ter, bet - ter, bet - ter, bet - ter, Oh! Da da da

da da da da da da da da, Hey___ Jude.

Repeat and Fade

I FEEL FINE

Words and Music by JOHN LENNON
and PAUL McCARTNEY

Bright rock tempo

Ba - by's good to me, you know,_ She's hap - py as can
Ba - by says she's mine, you know,_ She tells me all can the

be, you know,_ She said so;_ I'm in love with
time, you know,_ She said so;_

her and I__ feel fine.___ I'm so

(D.C.)

glad that she's my lit - tle girl, She's so

glad she's tell-ing all the world That her ba - by buys her

things, you know,_ He buys her dia - mond rings, you know,_ she said so;_

_ She's in love with me and I_ feel

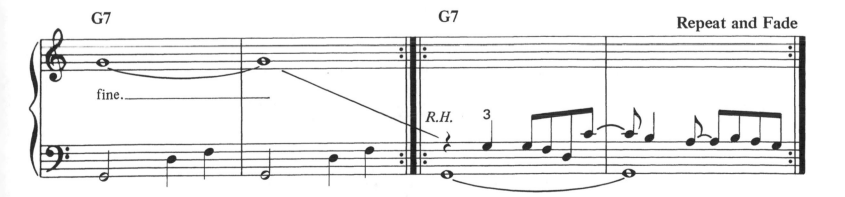

fine._

HELP!

Words and Music by JOHN LENNON
and PAUL McCARTNEY

Moderately, in 2 (♩ = 1 beat)

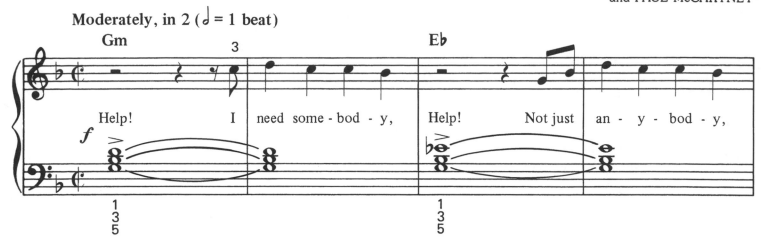

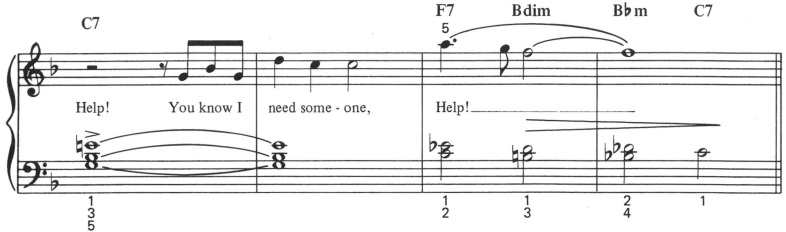

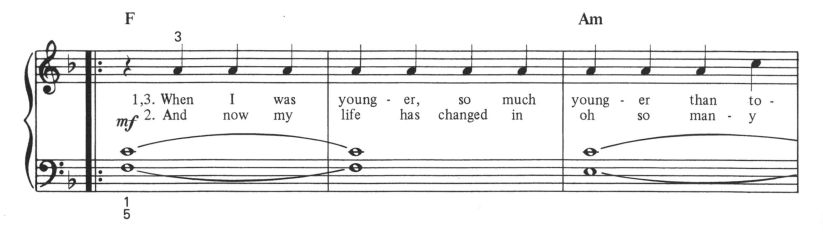

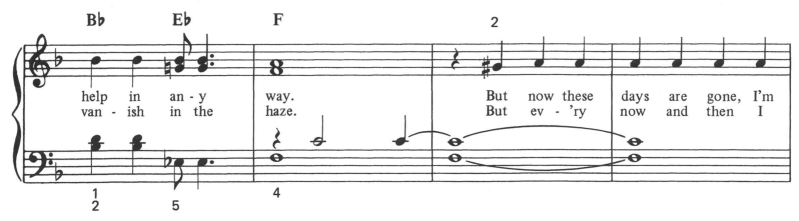

help in an-y way.
van-ish in the haze.
But now these days are gone, I'm
But ev-'ry now and then I

not so self as - sured,_____
feel so in - se - cure,_____
Now I find I've
I know that I just

changed my mind,
need you like
I've o - pened up the
I've nev - er done be - doors.
fore.

Help me if you can, I'm feel - ing down,_____ And I

do ap - pre - ci - ate you be - ing 'round.___

Help me get my feet back on the ground;___ Won't you

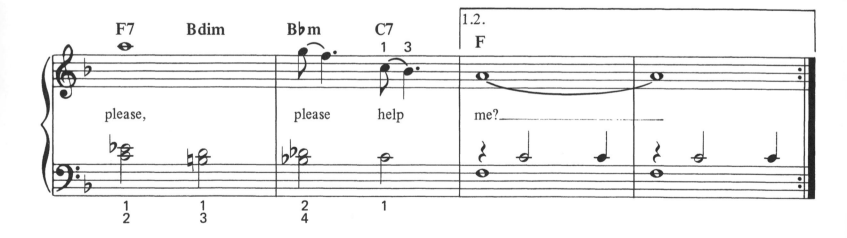

please, please help

me?___

me? Help me! Help me,___ oo!

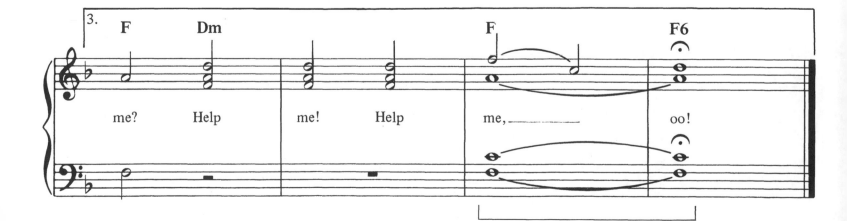

I WANT TO HOLD YOUR HAND

Words and Music by JOHN LENNON
and PAUL McCARTNEY

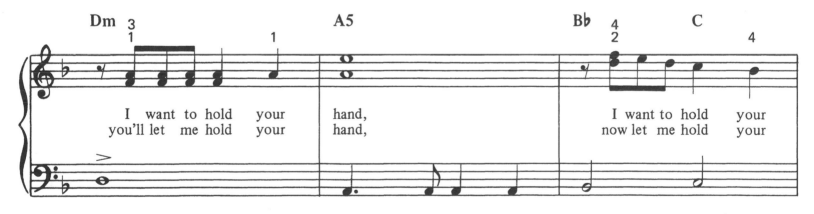

MCA MUSIC PUBLISHING

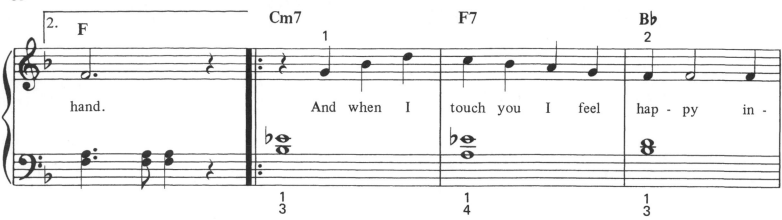

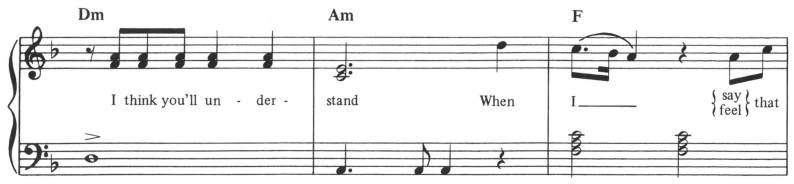

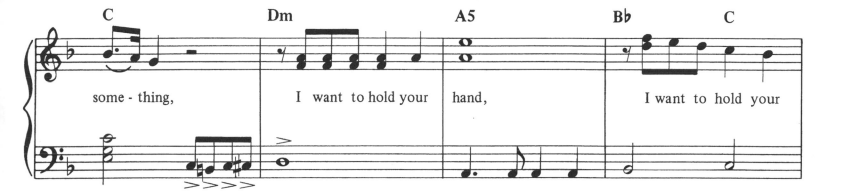

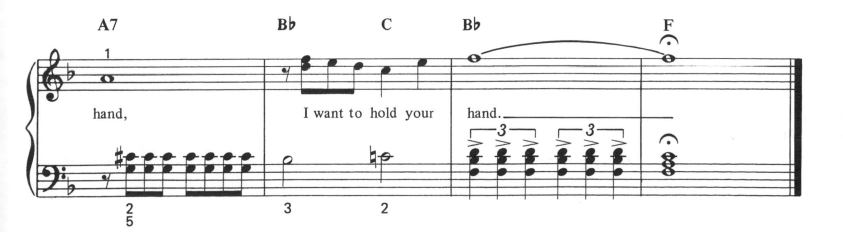

LADY MADONNA

Brightly, with a beat
(in 2, ♩ = 1 beat)

Words and Music by JOHN LENNON
and PAUL McCARTNEY

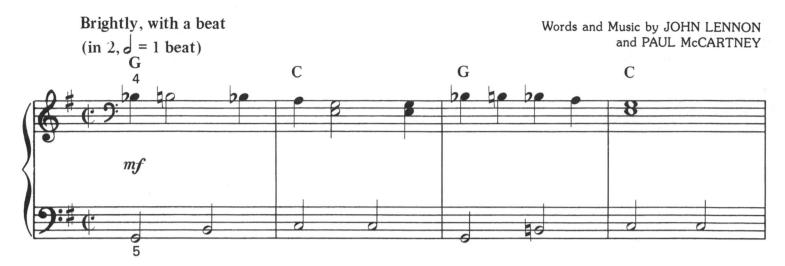

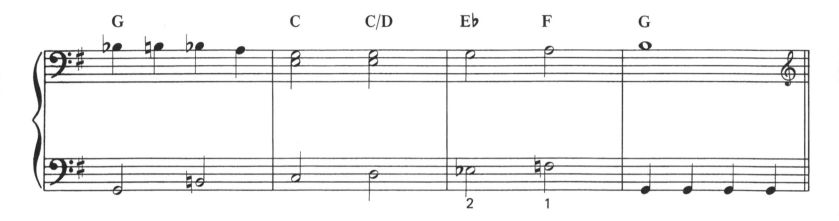

La - dy Ma - don - na, chil - dren at your feet,
La - dy Ma - don - na, ba - by at your breast,
La - dy Ma - don - na, chil - dren at your feet,

Last time to Coda ⊕

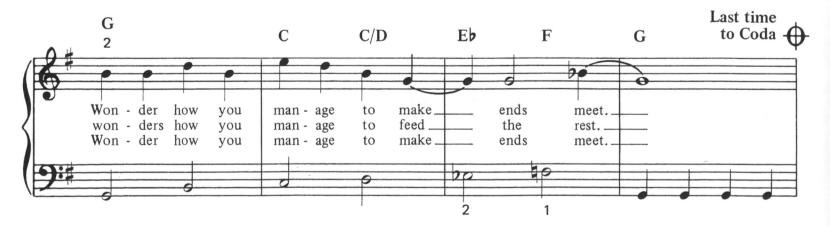

Won - der how you man - age to make___ ends meet.___
won - ders how you man - age to feed___ the rest.___
Won - der how you man - age to make___ ends meet.___

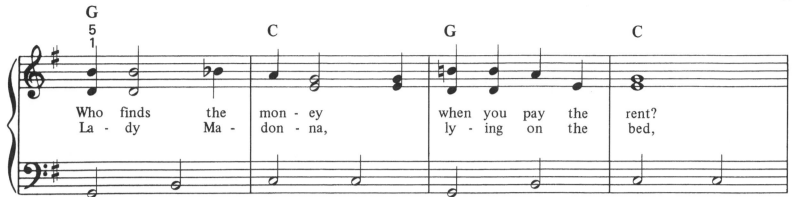

Who finds the mon - ey when you pay the rent?
La - dy Ma - don - na, ly - ing on the bed,

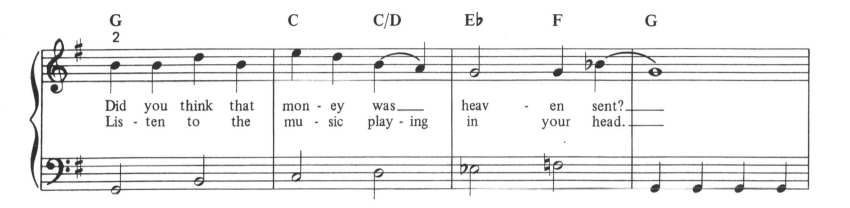

Did you think that mon - ey was____ heav - en sent?____
Lis - ten to the mu - sic play - ing in your head.____

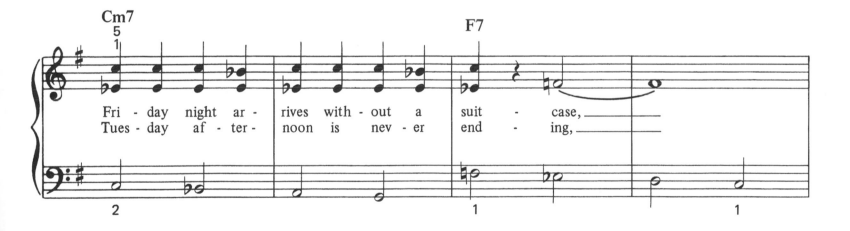

Fri - day night ar - rives with - out a suit - case,____
Tues - day af - ter - noon is nev - er end - ing,____

Sun - day morn - ing creep - ing like a nun.____
Wednes-day morn - ing pa - pers did - n't come.____

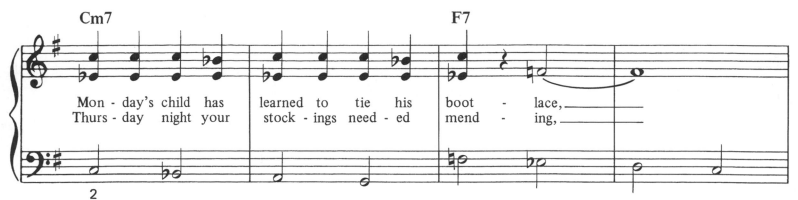

Mon - day's child has learned to tie his boot - lace,___
Thurs - day night your stock - ings need - ed mend - ing,___

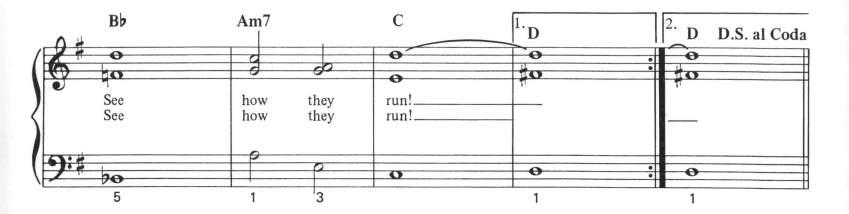

See how they run!___
See how they run!___

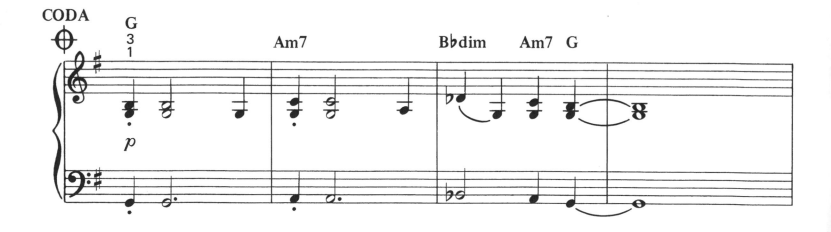

CODA

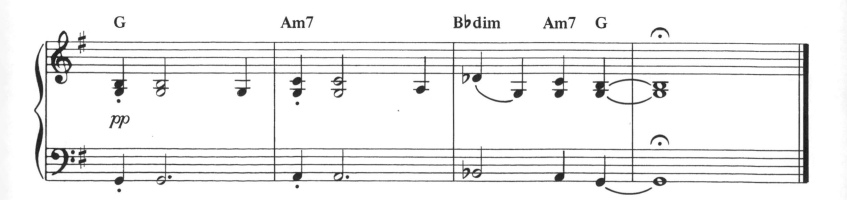

PAPERBACK WRITER

Words and Music by JOHN LENNON
and PAUL McCARTNEY

Bright rock beat

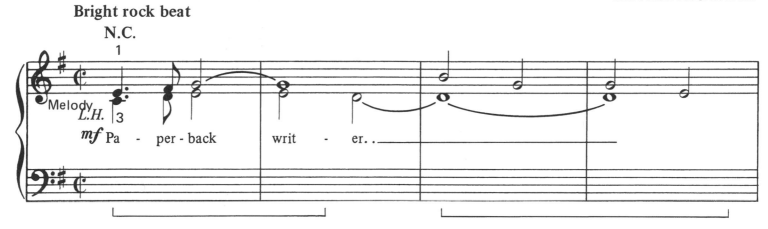

Melody
L.H.

Pa - per - back writ - er...

Dear___
It's a

Sir or Mad - am, will you read my book? It took me years to write, will you
thou - sand pag - es, give or take a few, I'll be writ - ing more in a

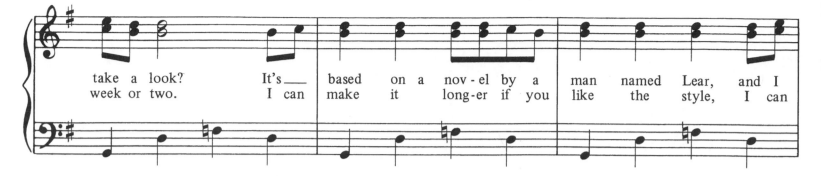

take a look? It's___ based on a nov-el by a man named Lear, and I
week or two. I can make it long-er if you like named the style, I can

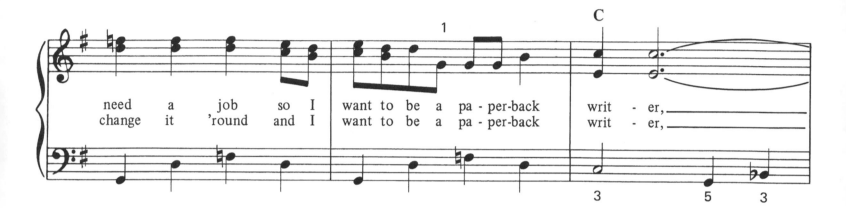

need a job so I want to be a pa-per-back writ - er,_____
change it 'round and I want to be a pa-per-back writ - er,_____

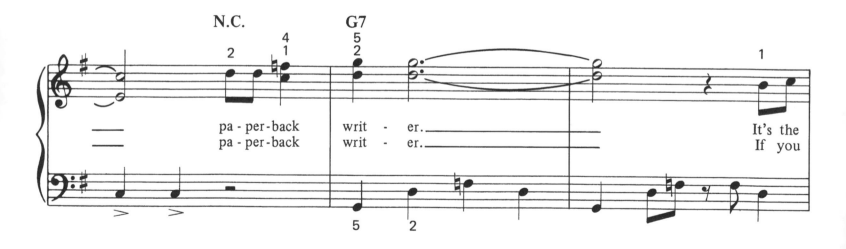

N.C.   G7
pa - per-back writ - er._____
pa - per-back writ - er._____   It's the
                                                     If you

dirt - y sto-ry of a dirt - y man,___ and his cling - ing wife does-n't
real - ly like it you can have the right,___ it could make a mil - lion for you

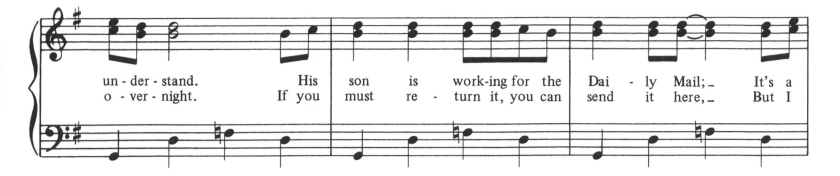

un-der-stand. His son is work-ing for the Dai - ly Mail; It's a
o - ver - night. If you must re - turn it, you can send it here, But I

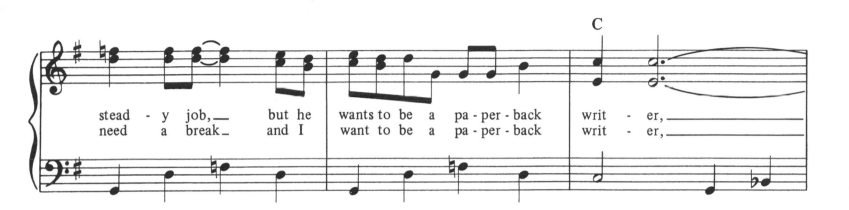

C

stead - y job, but he wants to be a pa-per-back writ - er,
need a break and I want to be a pa-per-back writ - er,

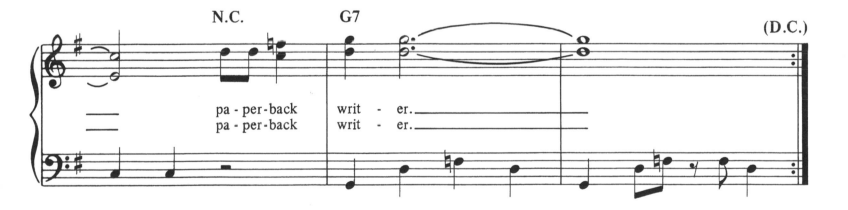

N.C.　　G7　　(D.C.)

pa-per-back writ - er.
pa-per-back writ - er.

G7　　Repeat and Fade

Pa - per-back writ - er...

LET IT BE

Words and Music by JOHN LENNON
and PAUL McCARTNEY

Slowly, in 2 (♩ = 1 beat)

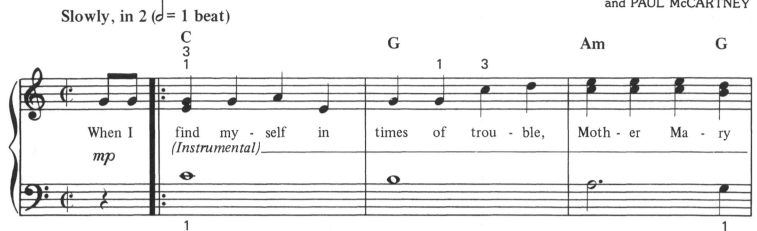

When I find my-self in times of trou-ble, Moth-er Ma-ry
mp *(Instrumental)*

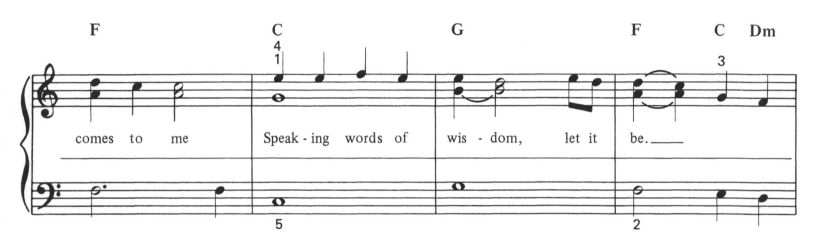

comes to me Speak-ing words of wis-dom, let it be.

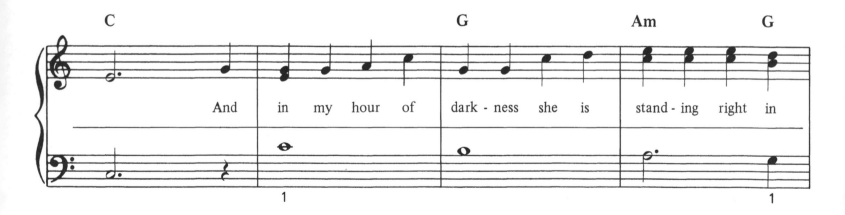

And in my hour of dark-ness she is stand-ing right in

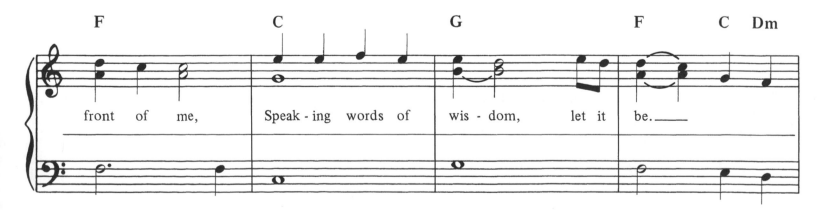

front of me, Speak-ing words of wis-dom, let it be.

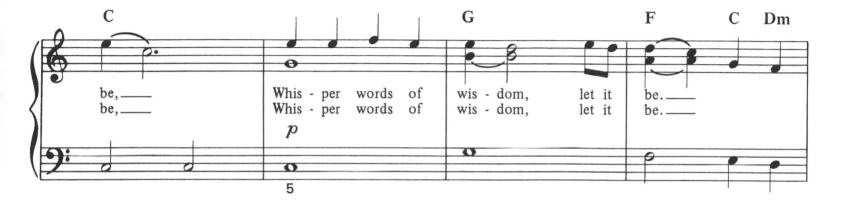

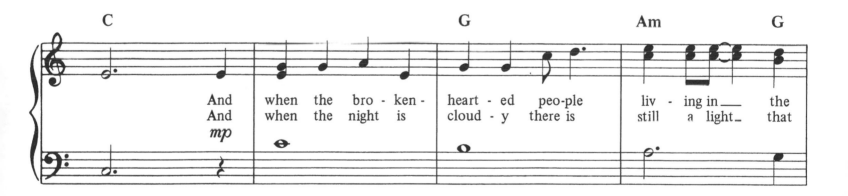

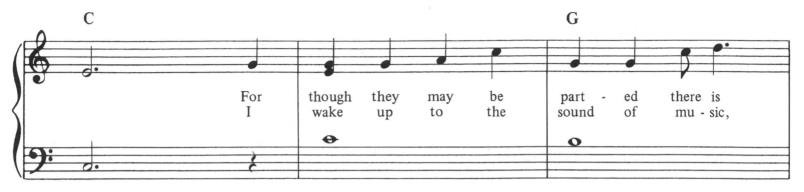

For though they may be parted there is
I wake up to the sound of music,

still a chance that they will see,
Moth - er Ma - ry comes to me,

There will be an
Speak-ing words of

an - swer, let it be.
wis - dom, let it be.

Let it be, let it

be, let it be, let it be,

There will be an

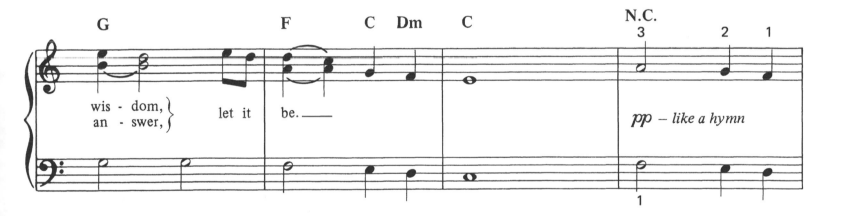

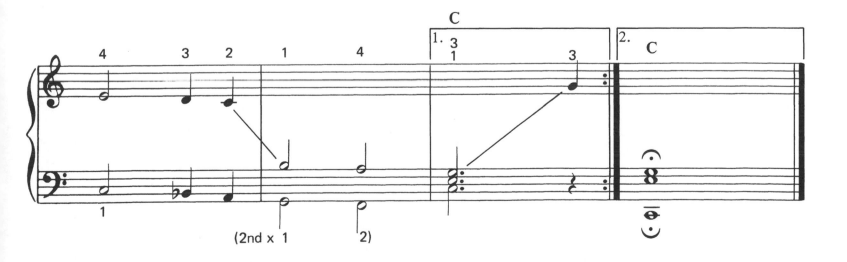

THE LONG AND WINDING ROAD

Words and Music by JOHN LENNON
and PAUL McCARTNEY

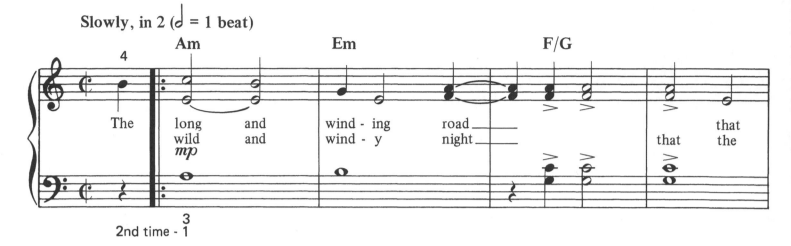

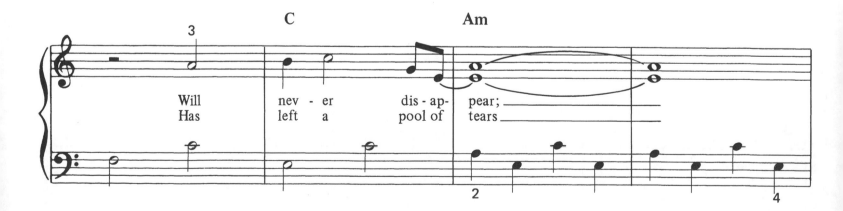

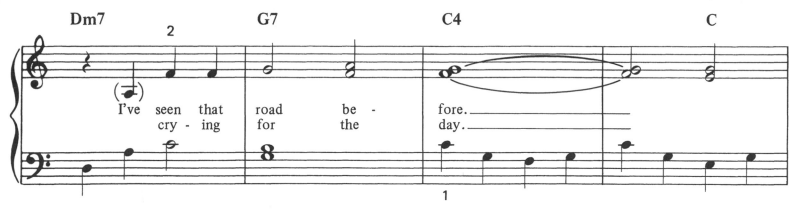

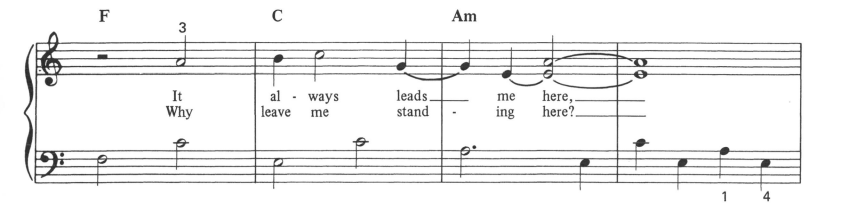

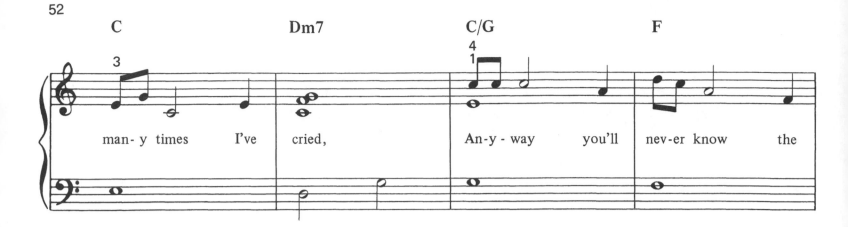

man-y times I've cried, An-y-way you'll nev-er know the

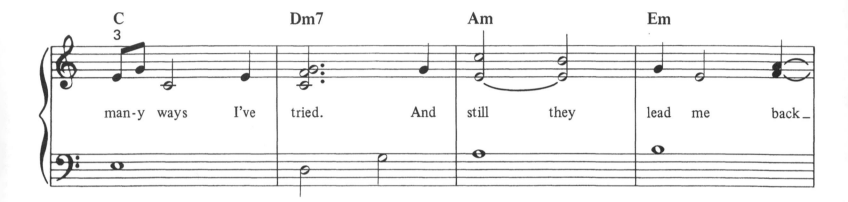

man-y ways I've tried. And still they lead me back

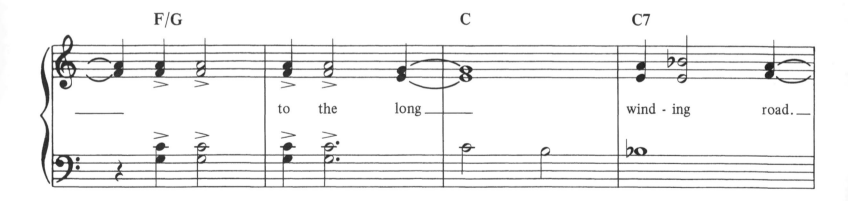

to the long wind-ing road.

You left me stand-ing

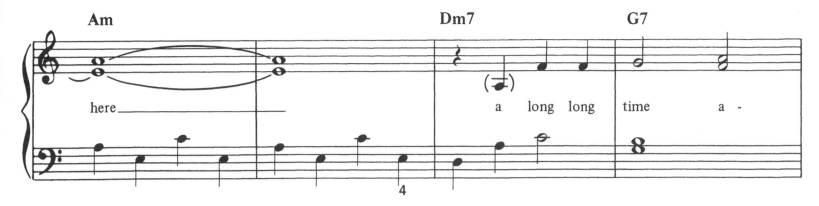

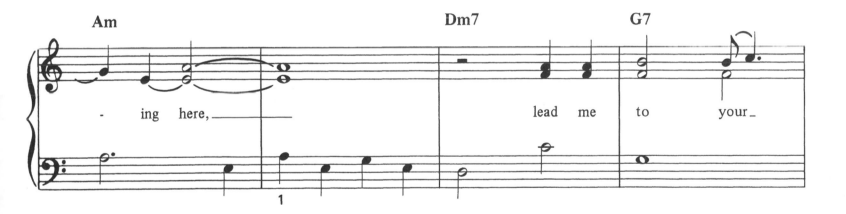

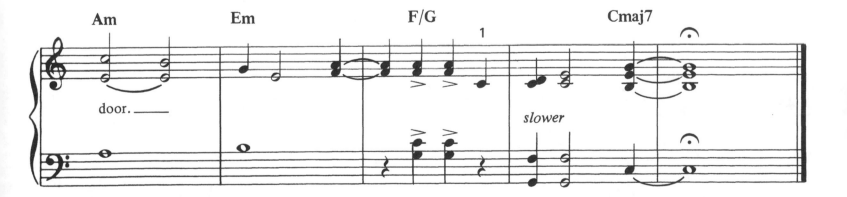

LOVE ME DO

Words and Music by PAUL McCARTNEY
and JOHN LENNON

Moderate Rock

Love, love me do,___ you know I love you,___ I'll

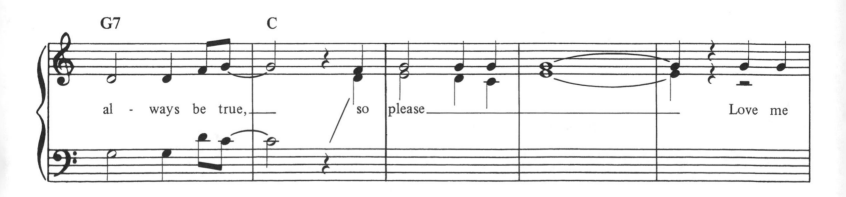

al - ways be true,___ so please___ Love me

PENNY LANE

Words and Music by JOHN LENNON
and PAUL McCARTNEY

With a lilting beat

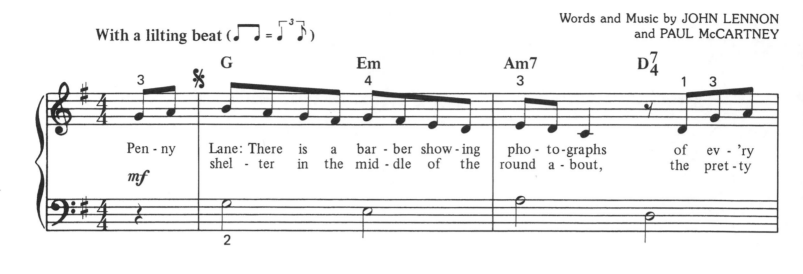

Pen - ny Lane: There is a bar - ber show - ing the pho - to - graphs of ev - 'ry
shel - ter in the mid - dle of the round a - bout, the pret - ty

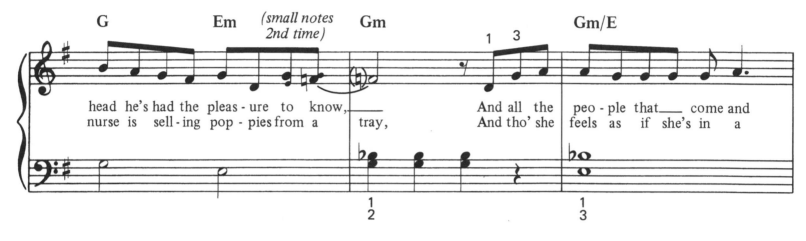

head he's had the pleas - ure to know, And all the peo - ple that___ come and
nurse is sell - ing pop - pies from a tray, And tho' she feels as if she's in a

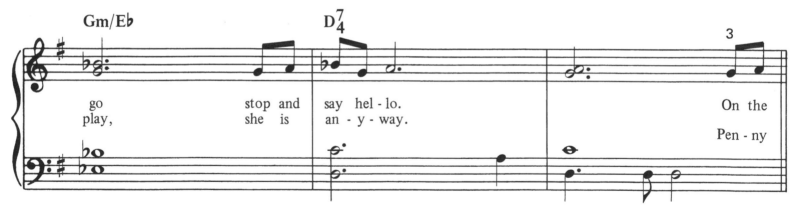

go stop and say hel - lo. On the
play, she is an - y - way. Pen - ny

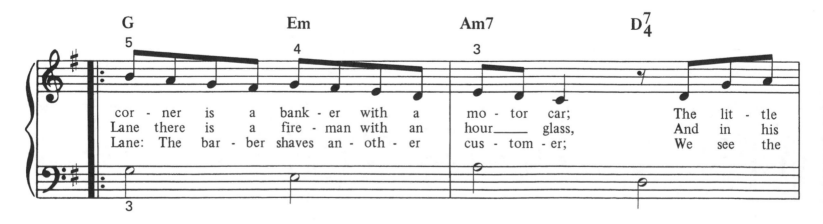

cor - ner is a bank - er with a mo - tor car; The lit - tle
Lane there is a fire - man with an hour___ glass, And in his
Lane: The bar - ber shaves an - oth - er cus - tom - er; We see the

chil - dren laugh at him be - hind his back. And the
pock - et is a por - trait of the Queen. He likes to
bank - er sit - ting wait - ing for a trim. And then the

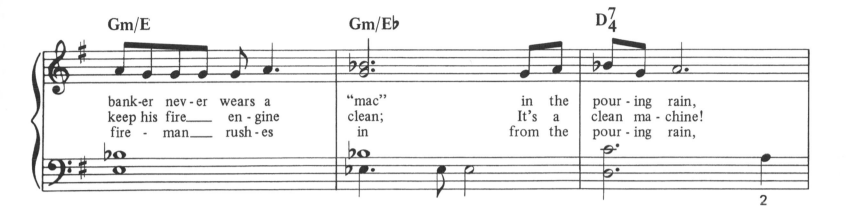

bank-er nev-er wears a "mac" in the pour-ing rain,
keep his fire___ en - gine clean; It's a clean ma - chine!
fire - man___ rush - es in from the pour-ing rain,

ver - y strange! Pen-ny Lane is in my ears and in my
Pen-ny Lane is in my ears and in my
ver - y strange! Pen-ny Lane is in my ears and in my

eyes,___ Wet be - neath the
eyes,___ full of
eyes,___ there be - neath the

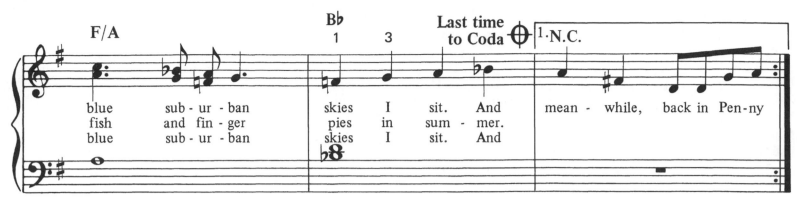

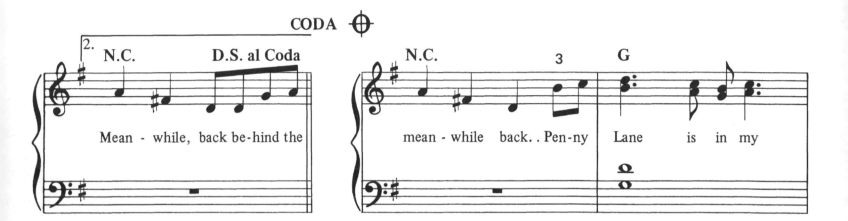

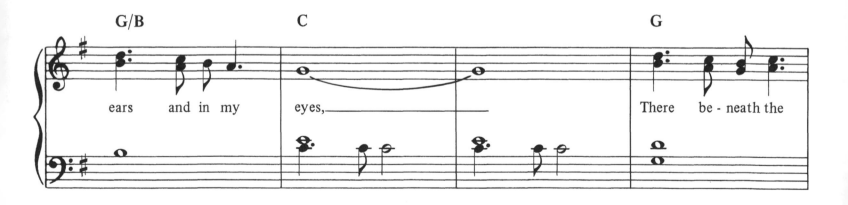

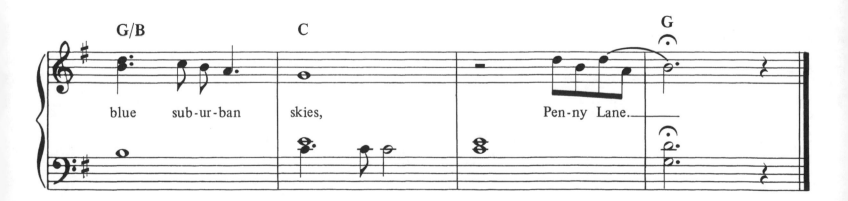

PLEASE PLEASE ME

Words by JOHN LENNON
and PAUL McCARTNEY

Moderate Rock

1.3. Last night I said these words to my girl,
2. You don't need me to show the way, love,

I know you/I nev-er e-ven
Why do I al-ways have to

try, girl.
say, love,

Come on (Come on ___) Come

on (Come on ___) Come on (Come on ___) Come on (Come on ___) Please,

please me, wo yeah, like I please you.

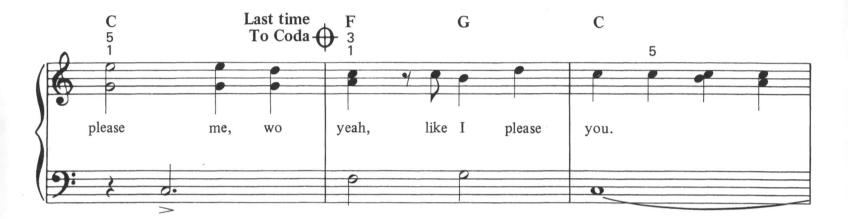

I don't want to sound com-plain-ing

but you know there's al - ways rain in my ___ heart.

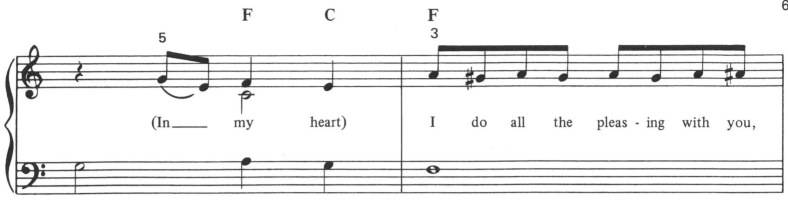

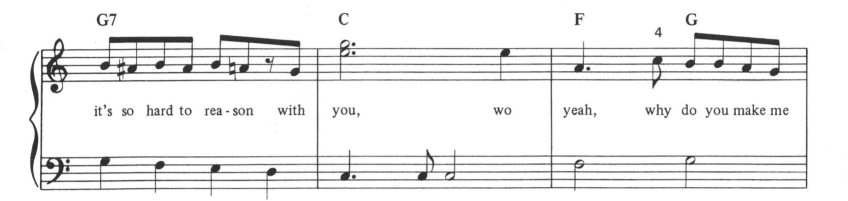

SHE LOVES YOU

Words by JOHN LENNON
and PAUL McCARTNEY

Brisk rock tempo

She loves you yeah, yeah, yeah, She loves you, yeah,

yeah, yeah, She loves you, yeah, yeah, yeah, yeah.____

____ You think you've lost your love? Well, I saw her yes-ter-

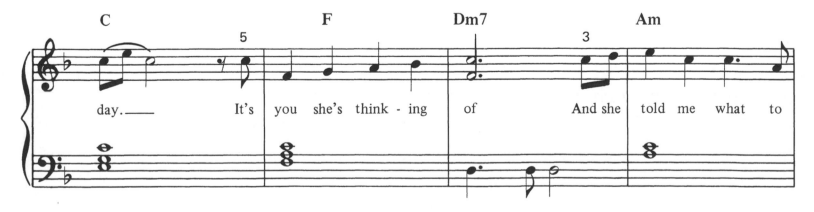

day.____ It's you she's think-ing of And she told me what to

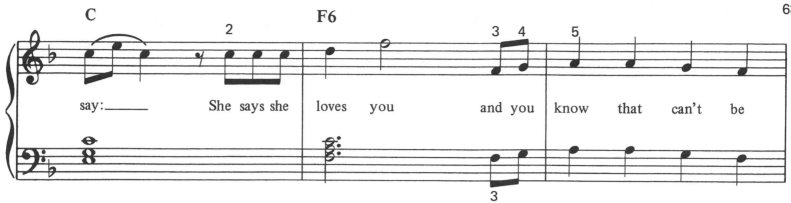

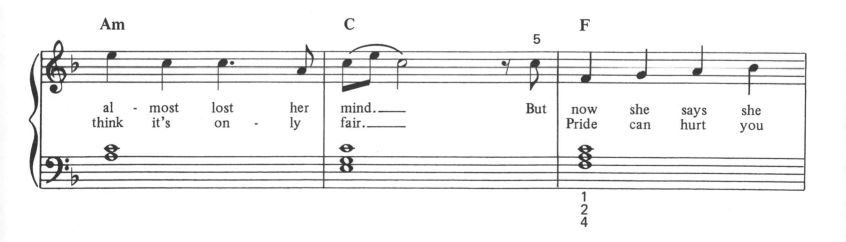

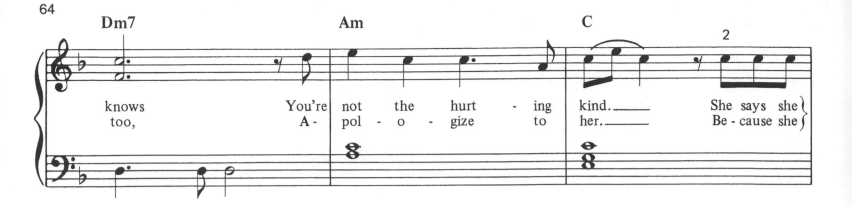

knows / too, You're / A- not / pol the / o hurt / gize ing / to kind. / her. She says she / Be - cause she

loves you and you know that can't be bad. Yes, she

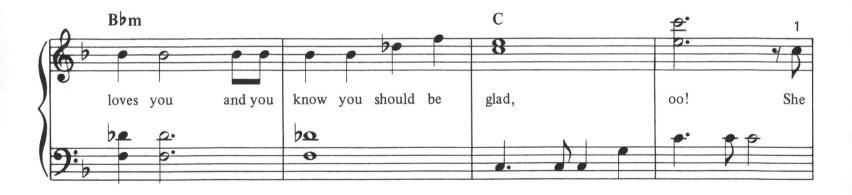

loves you and you know you should be glad, oo! She

loves you, yeah, yeah, yeah, She loves you, yeah,

yeah,   yeah. And with a love   like   that   you   know   you   should   be

glad._____ You glad,_____ With a

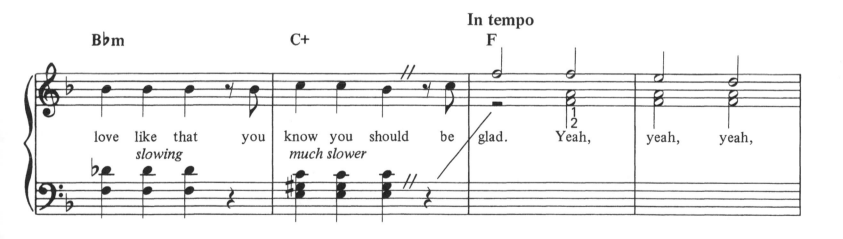

love   like   that   you   know you should   be   glad.   Yeah,   yeah,   yeah,

slowing   *much slower*

yeah,   yeah,   yeah,   yeah,   yeah,   yeah,   yeah!

SOMETHING

Words and Music by
GEORGE HARRISON

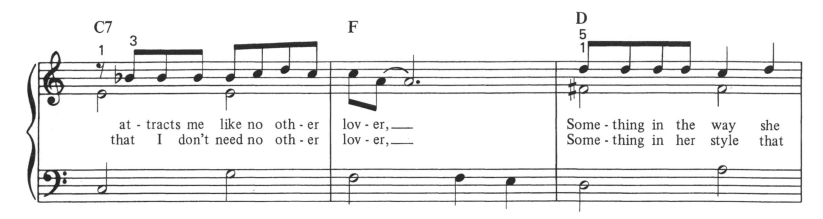

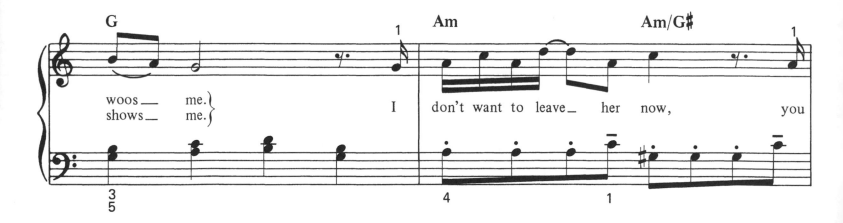

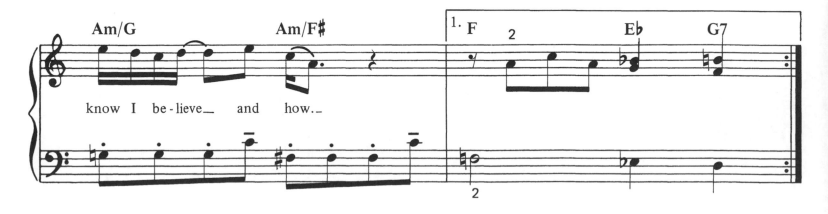

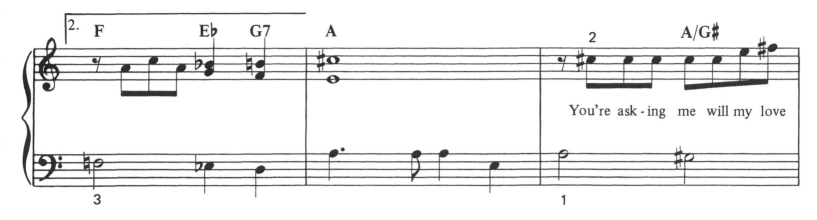

You're ask-ing me will my love

grow? I don't know,___ I don't know.

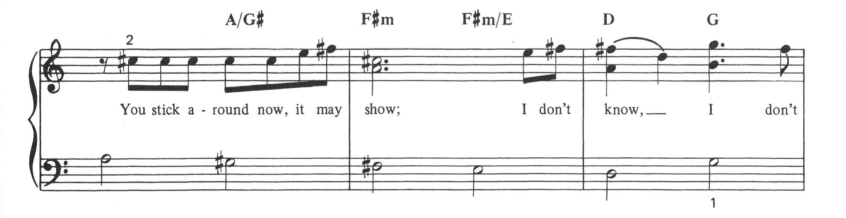

You stick a-round now, it may show; I don't know,___ I don't

know. Some-thing in the way she knows,___

and all I have to do is think of her. Some-thing in the things she

shows __ me, I don't want to leave __ her now, you

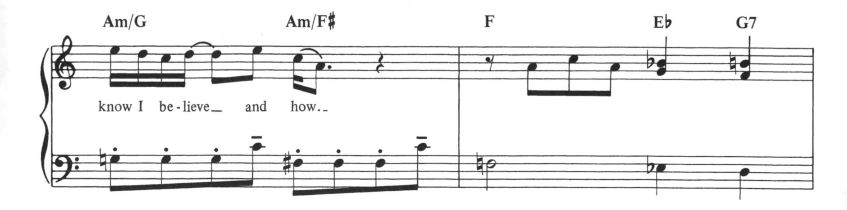

know I be-lieve __ and how..

TICKET TO RIDE

Words and Music by JOHN LENNON
and PAUL McCARTNEY

Moderate Rock

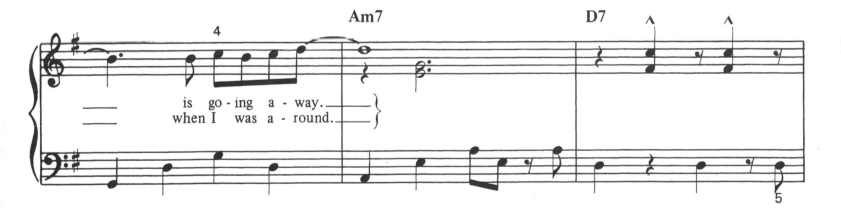

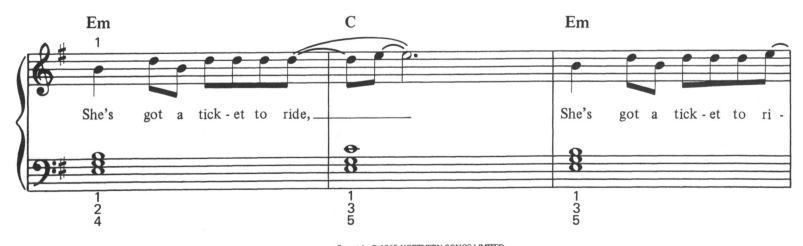

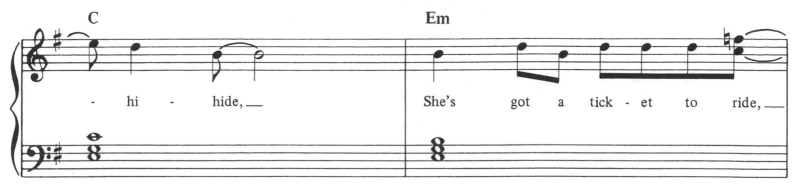

- hi - hide, ___ She's got a tick - et to ride, ___

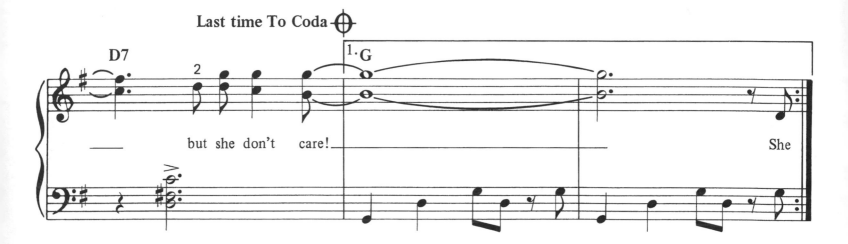

Last time To Coda ⊕

___ but she don't care! ___ She

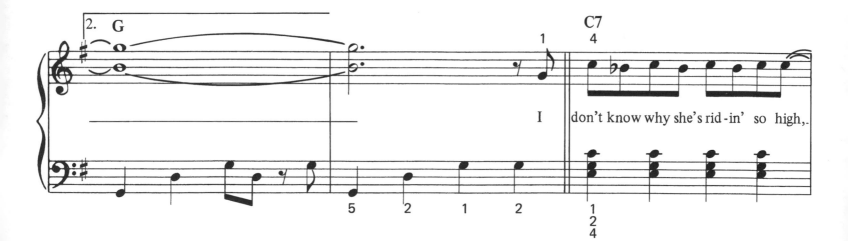

I don't know why she's rid -in' so high, ___

she ought - ta think twice she ought-ta do right by

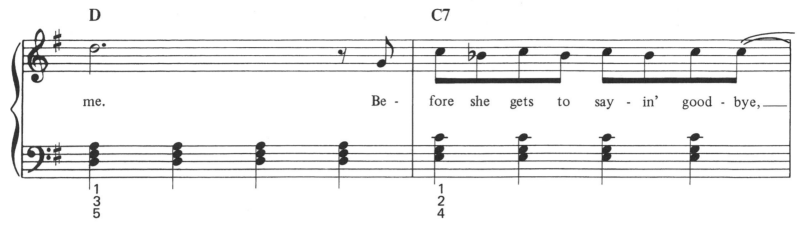

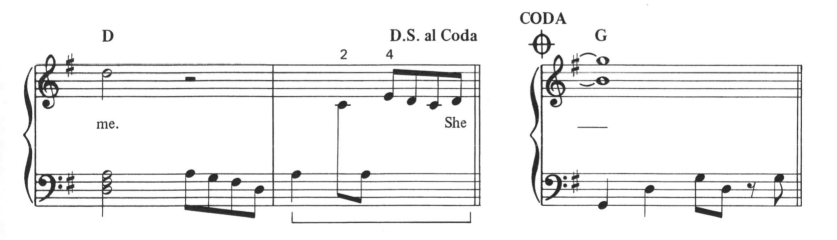

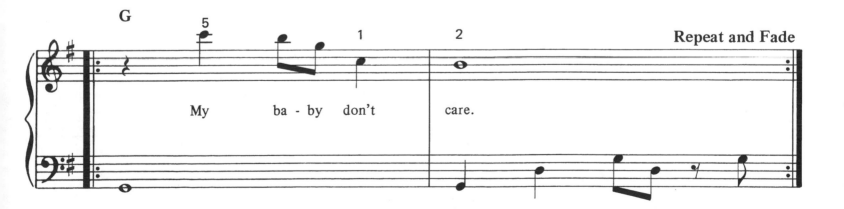

YESTERDAY

Words and Music by JOHN LENNON
and PAUL McCARTNEY

Moderately, with expression

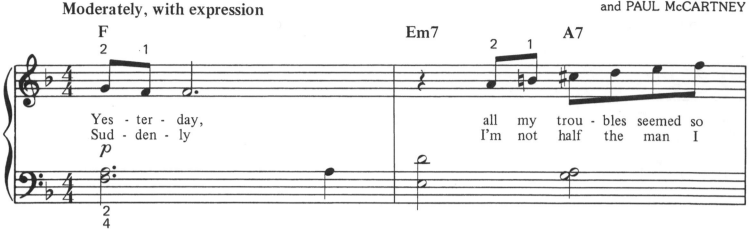

Yes - ter - day,
Sud - den - ly

all my trou - bles seemed so
I'm not half the man I

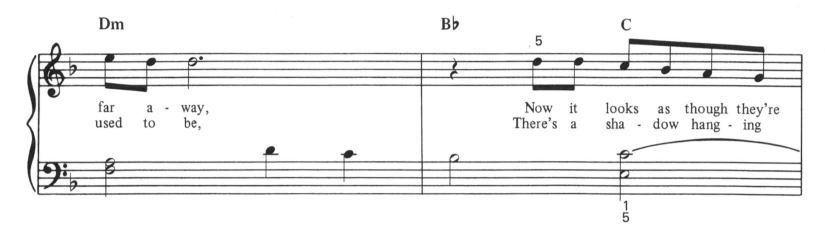

far a - way,
used to be,

Now it looks as though they're
There's a sha - dow hang - ing

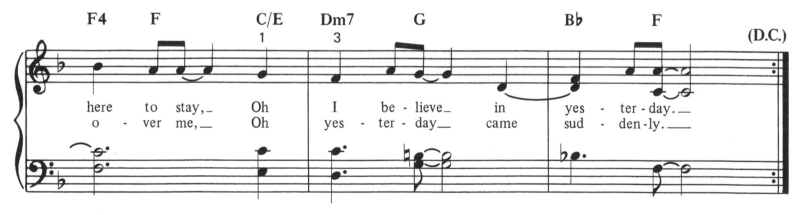

here to stay,__ Oh
o - ver me,__ Oh

I be - lieve__ in yes - ter - day.__
yes - ter - day__ came sud - den - ly.__

(D.C.)

Why she had to go I don't know, she would - n't say.

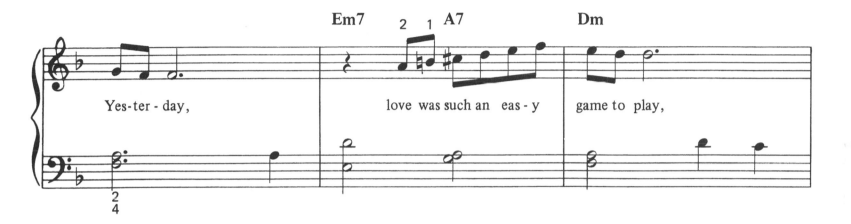

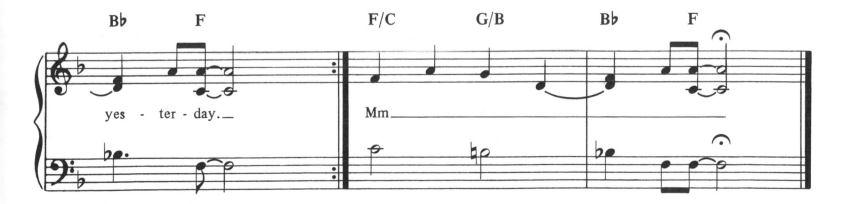

WE CAN WORK IT OUT

Words and Music by JOHN LENNON
and PAUL McCARTNEY

Slow and Steady

Try to see it, my way,
mf Think of what you're say - ing,
do I have to keep on talk - ing
you can get it wrong and still you

till I can't go on?
think that it's all right.
While you see it your way,
Think of what I'm say - ing,

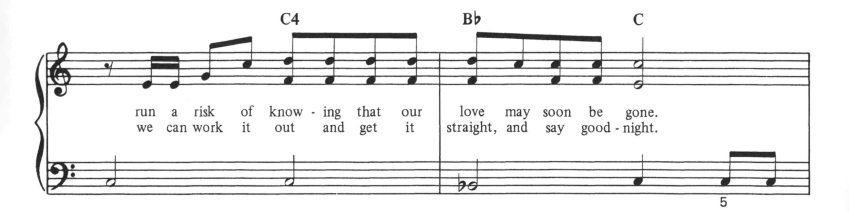

run a risk of know - ing that our
we can work it out and get it
love may soon be gone.
straight, and say good - night.

We can work it out,
we can work it out._____

(D.C.)

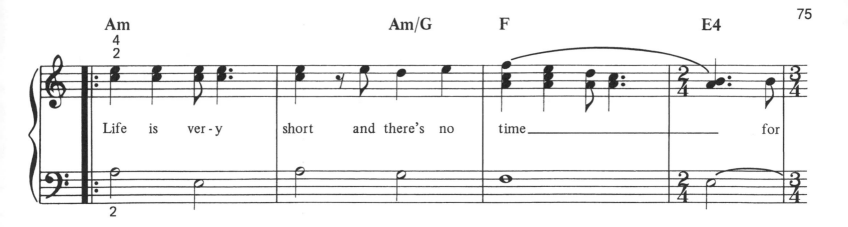

Life is ver-y short and there's no time____ for

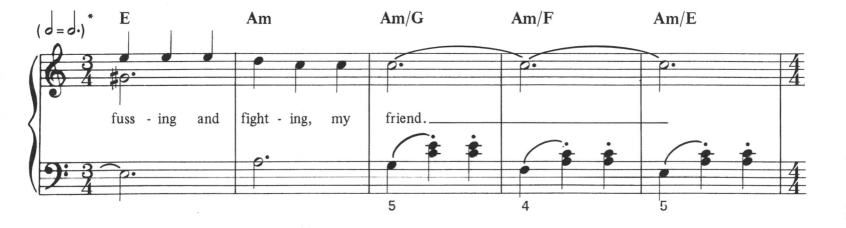

fuss - ing and fight - ing, my friend.____

I have al - ways thought that it's a crime____ so I will

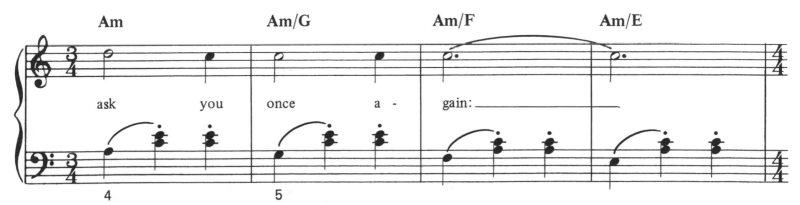

ask you once a - gain:____

*Each 3/4 measure played in the same amount of time as the previous 2/4 measure.

Try to see it my way, on-ly time will tell if I am right or I am wrong.

While you see it your way there's a chance that we might fall a-

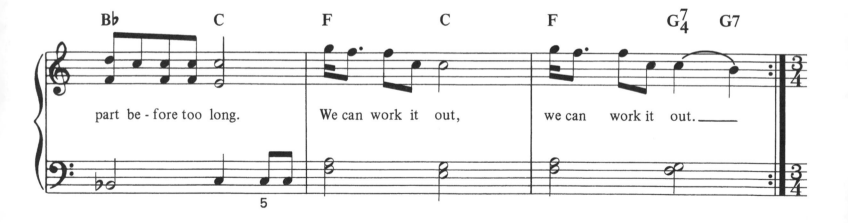

part be-fore too long. We can work it out, we can work it out.____

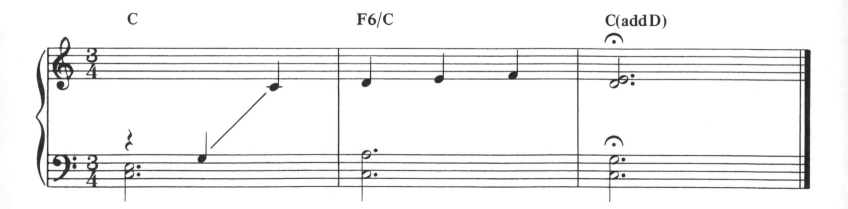

GET BACK

Words and Music by JOHN LENNON
and PAUL McCARTNEY

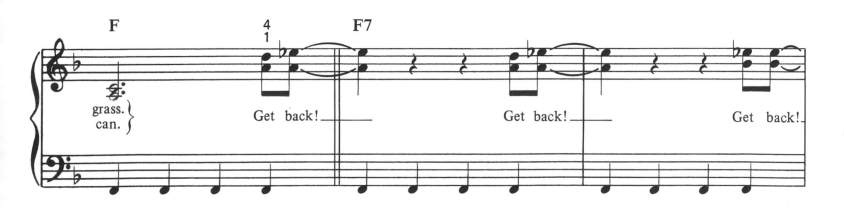

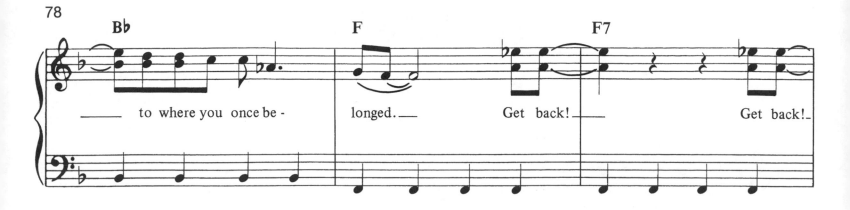

Repeat and Fade